Kids' Book of
Brain
Boosting
Puzzles

ARCTURUS

ARCTURUS

This edition published in 2023 by Arcturus Publishing Limited
26/27 Bickels Yard, 151–153 Bermondsey Street,
London SE1 3HA

Author: Ivy Finnegan
Illustrator: Andrea Castro Naranjo
Designer: Trudi Webb
Editors: Donna Gregory and Rebecca Razo
Design Manager: Jessica Holliland
Editorial Manager: Joe Harris

ISBN: 978-1-3988-2596-3
CH010426NT
Supplier 29, Date 0423, PI 00002691

Printed in China

Brain-Boosting Tips

Do you love matching pairs, spotting differences, and working out clues to solve problems? Exercise your brain and have fun at the same time with the awesome activities in this interactive book! Here are some helpful tips to bear in mind as you go along:

• Read the introduction to each puzzle carefully so you know what to do—sometimes it helps to read it out loud.

• If you get stuck, you can always leave a puzzle and come back to it later.

• When you're ready to check your answers, you'll find them starting on page 87.
(No peeking—unless you get really stuck, of course!)

Ready to get started?

Grab a pencil, turn the page, and start boosting your brain!

Which Witch?

Can you spot the 10 differences between these two spooky scenes?

Knight Vision

In what order do these panels belong?
Write their correct numbers, from left to right.

Bounty Aplenty

Can you match these pirates with their treasure troves?
Each is wearing an item identical to one in their collection.

Just Kitten Around

Each of these mother cats has kittens that look just like her. Can you work out how many kittens belong to each mother? How many kittens are there in total?

Feeding Time

Which of the tiles below does not appear in this picture?

A   B   C   D

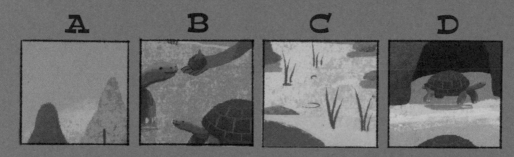

Messy Mer-Kids

These mer-twins have dropped some of their possessions. All of their things—shown at the top of the page—are somewhere in this scene. Can you find them?

Waggy-Tail Walkers

Can you match each dog to its human?

Beetling About

Which beetle is not an exact match to the others?

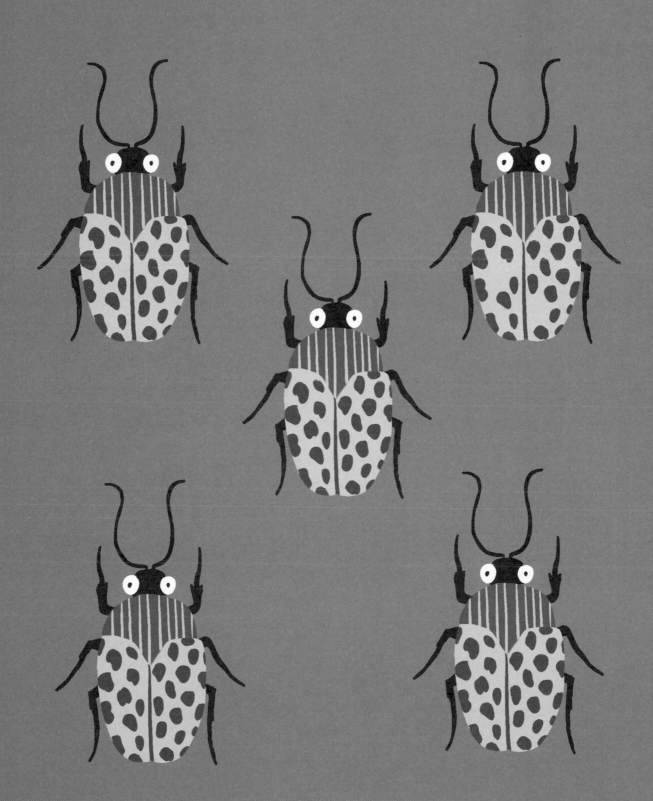

Putting Down Roots

Each of these forest workers takes 15 minutes to plant one tree.
How many trees will the three of them plant in seven hours?

Diving In

In what order do these panels belong? Write their correct numbers, from left to right.

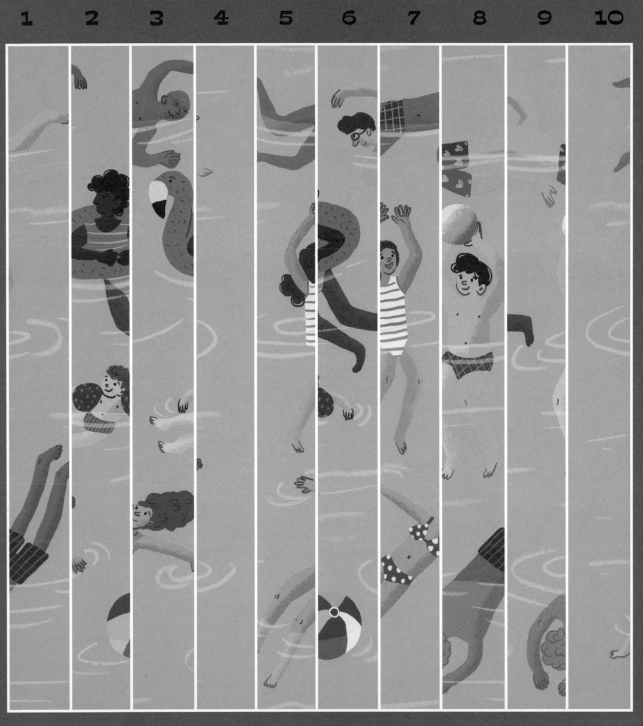

Toy Store Stumper

Can you help this worker sort the toys in the grid below? Place one toy into each empty square so that every horizontal row and vertical column contains six different objects. To help you, some of them are already in place.

Model Mayhem

This engineer wants to look at the model for her roof, but she needs to find the right one first. Can you figure out which model matches her diagram?

Snow Much Fun

How many polar bears can you find
in this Arctic scene?

Puppy Pals

Each of these kids has a pet dog. Can you work out which dog belongs to each child based on the clues provided below?

Asha

Juan

> My name is Asha. My dog has floppy ears and a long tail.
>
> My name is Juan. My dog has spots.
>
> My name is Ava. My dog has spots and pointed ears.
>
> My name is Ethan. My dog has pointed ears and a long tail.

Ava

Ethan

Alligator Snap

Which one of the tiles at the bottom of the page is not from this picture of alligators playing Snap?

1 2 3 4 5 6 7 8

Monkeying Around

Which silhouette matches this monkey family portrait exactly?

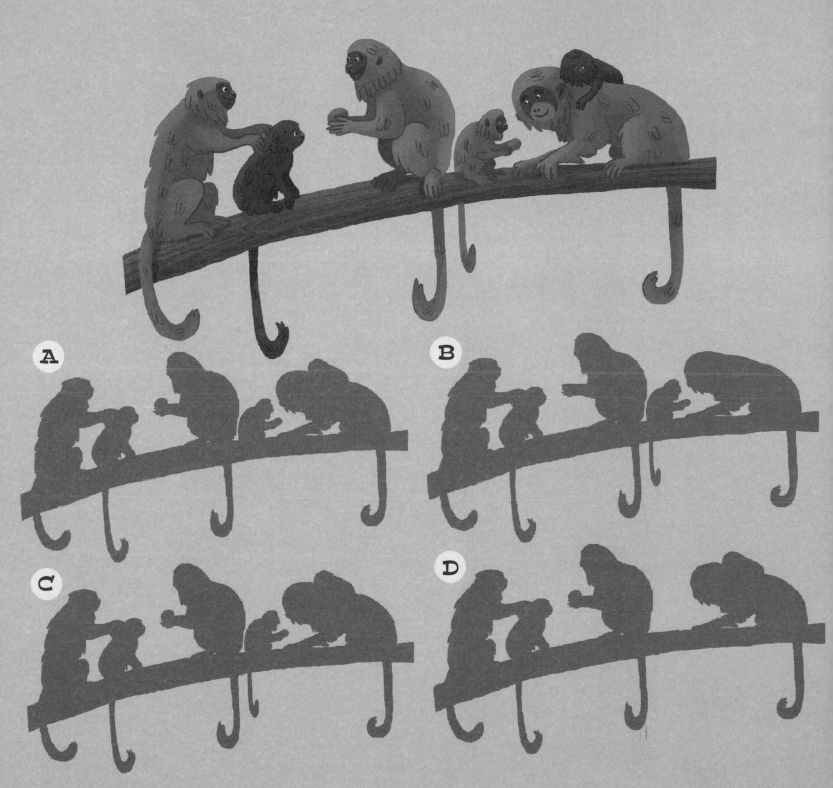

Penguin Pairs

Can you spot which two of these penguins aren't part of a pair?

Dragon's Nest

How many swords can you find in this dragon's treasure hoard?

River Rocks

Can you guide this conservationist safely over the river back to her boat? She can only go up, down, left, or right, not diagonally. She can start anywhere on the top row. She must step on the rocks in the order shown (brown, green, yellow).

Can You Dig It?

Which of these sets contains all of the parts of this archaeologist's equipment?

Adventure Bikes

Can you follow these twisting trails to find out
which kid lives in each house?

The Butterfly Effect

Use the clues below to help you find the six missing
butterfly youngsters.

One is a caterpillar and is three squares long.

Two are chrysalises and are each two squares long.

Three are eggs and only take up one square each.

The numbers in the grid tell you how many parts are in each row and column. None
of the youngsters are in touching squares, horizontally, vertically, or diagonally.

Wonderlost

Help Alice find her way back to the rabbit hole. Use the compass, key, and clues to work out what to do at each landmark. Your final destination is the location of the rabbit hole.

KEY
- Cheshire Cat tree
- Mushroom
- Playing card
- Potion bottle

Whenever you reach a mushroom, turn east.

Whenever you reach a playing card, turn south.

Whenever you reach a Cheshire Cat tree, turn north.

Whenever you reach a potion bottle, turn west.

START

Is the rabbit hole ...

in the Red Queen's palace?

in the Mad Hatter's house?

near the borogrove?

Cake Challenge

This baker's cake changes at each step. Can you work out what the pattern is and then fill in the final cake so it is the fifth in sequence?

Island Hopping

Complete the puzzle below by drawing lines to represent the paths taken by the boats from one island to another. You can only draw horizontal and vertical paths, and each island must have the same number of paths connecting to it as the number printed inside of it. Paths cannot cross over one another. The first island (number 3) has been connected so you can see how it works.

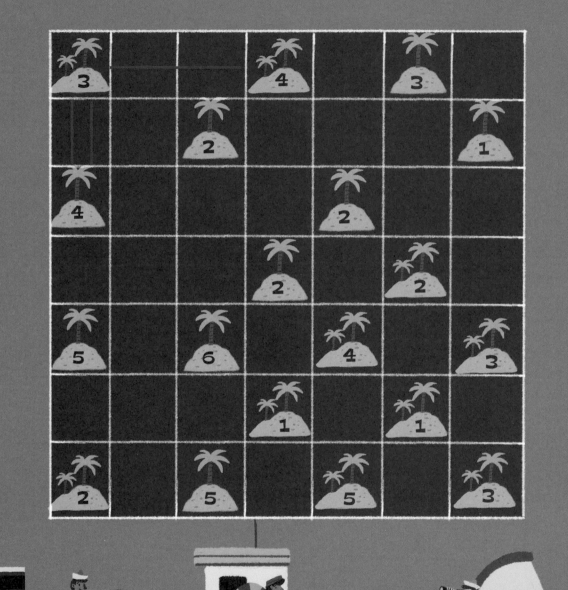

Crank it Up!

These engineers are building a new machine and need to figure out how the cogs interact with each other. If they start by turning the green cog clockwise, can you work out the directions the other cogs will turn in response? Each wheel turns in the opposite way to the one next to it. In what direction will the final pink cog turn?

Deep-Sea Spotting

Which jigsaw piece does not belong to this underwater scene?

Mayflies in Disguise

Can you find the mayfly that is slightly different
from the rest?

Puddle in the Muddle

Can you arrange the squares of this picture so they form a single completed image of a boy splashing a puddle? Write the numbers in the empty grid to show where each square should go. The first few have been done for you.

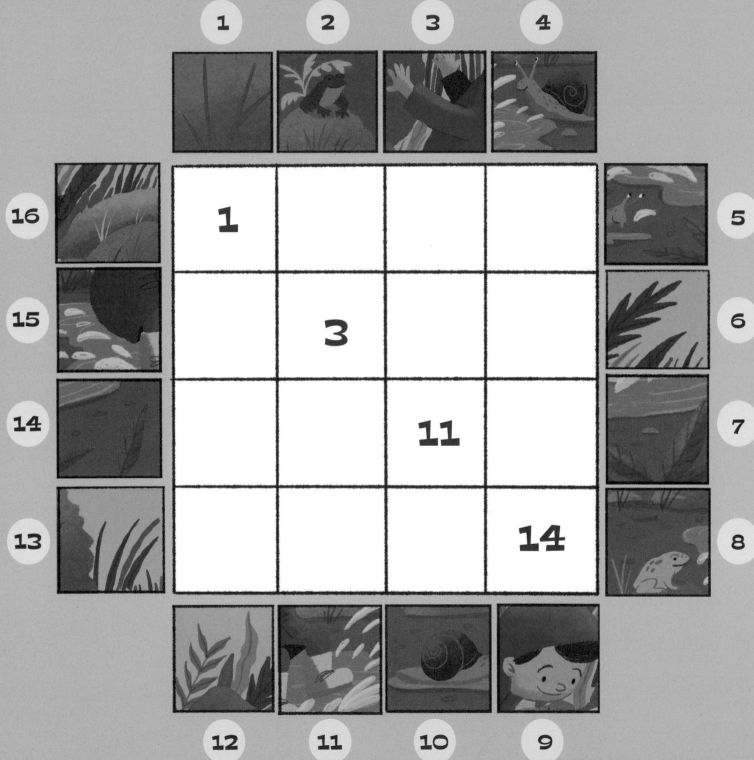

Mice Maze

These four mice are on the hunt for the sunflower so they can eat its seeds. Can you work out which mouse will get the sunflower?

Monster Mystery

Can you find all of the monsters in this grid? The numbers around the outside tell you how many monsters are in each row and column. A monster can only be found horizontally or vertically next to a cabin, and monsters are never positioned next to each other vertically, horizontally, or diagonally. One monster has been added to get you started.

Star Bright

How many stars can you count in the jumble below?

Put a Fork in It

The cutlery in this drawer got jumbled up, so the knives and forks are mixed together in each other's compartments. By taking a knife from one compartment and swapping it with a fork from the other compartment, what is the smallest number of swaps it would take to get all the knives in one compartment and all the forks in the other?

A Leg Up

How many combined legs do the creatures in this picture have?
Bees have six legs, spiders have eight legs, and birds have two legs.

Crowd Pleaser

Can you find this small group hiding
in the bigger crowd?

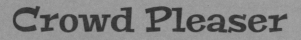

A Tall Order

Can you work out the order of these clowns from tallest to shortest starting at the tops of their heads? Keep an eye out for big hair and hats that make some of the clowns look taller than they really are!

Dress-Up Box

Which of these sets contains the correct
props that these actors are wearing or using?

We Have Bake-Off!

Nina, Kate, and Nico have each baked one of the following: a cupcake, a pie, and a layer cake. One chef has used strawberries, one chef has used lemons, and one has used chocolate. Use the clues to match the finished desserts to their baker and then figure out who used each ingredient.

Kate's dish is larger than Nico's.

Nico did not use lemons.

The strawberry dish is the smallest.

Nico's dish is not the smallest.

Nina   Kate   Nico

Tiaras in a Tangle

How many royal tiaras can you count
in the tangle below?

Pairing Up

Can you spot the only shoe in this picture that isn't part of a pair?

Track Stars

In what order do these panels belong?
Write their correct numbers, from left to right.

Busy Bees

Each of these flowers has a bee in a square directly next to it. Can you use these clues to mark all of the squares that have a bee in them? One has already been done for you.

A bee is always above, below, or to the side of a flower, but never diagonally adjacent.

Bees are not next to other bees, either horizontally, vertically, or diagonally.

The numbers alongside the grid show how many bees are in each row and column.

Bounce Out

Can you find this group of balls in the grid below?

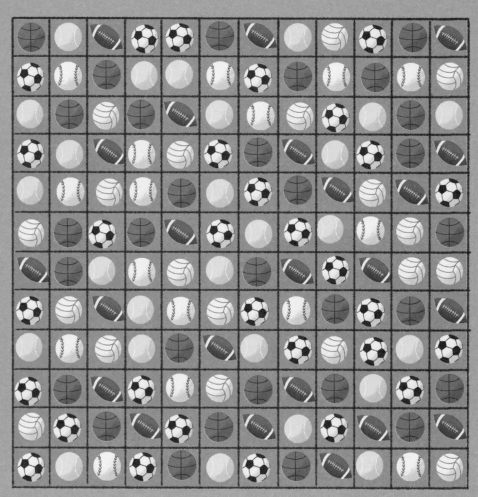

Day at the Museum

Can you spot the eight differences between these two family photos?

Fungi Fun

The spots of each of the toadstools form a sequence. Can you complete the pattern by drawing the correct number of spots on the final toadstool in each row?

Smitten Kitten

Which ball of yarn is the kitten playing with?

Maximum Load

This fairy's tractor can only fly with a load that weighs less than 15 feathers. Using the clues below, can you work out which pile her tractor can pull?

Each flower bunch weighs two feathers.

Each ginger weighs one feather.

Each bale of dandelion fluff weighs four feathers.

1

2

3

Munch a Bunch

Can you help the caterpillars finish the patterns they've been making in these leaves? Each group of four leaves forms a sequence, but the caterpillars haven't finished the fourth leaf yet. Can you work out the sequence and fill in the missing holes?

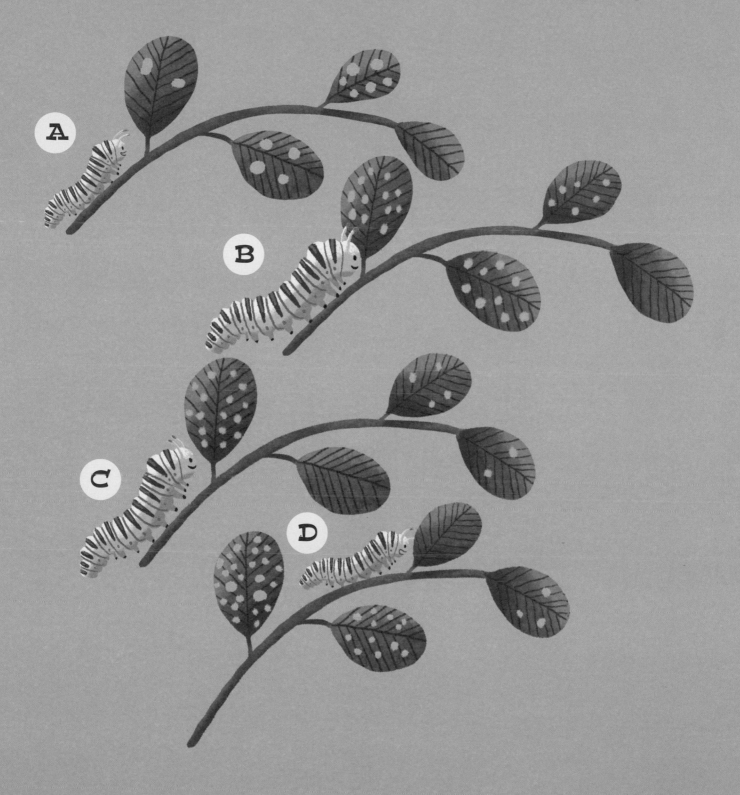

Pizzarithmetic

This oven can cook four pizzas every 12 minutes.
How long will it take to cook 17 pizzas if the oven can
cook four pizzas at one time?

Bangle Tangle

How many bracelets can you count in the tangle below?

Banking Error

This banker has mixed up the safety deposit box keys with their labels. Can you help her work out which key goes with each label so the banker can put the labels back on? Which key is still missing a label?

Entry Code

To open the door to her top-secret laboratory, this scientist
needs to find the pattern that matches the one on her tablet.
Can you help her spot it?

Pizza the Action

Louise, Marta, and Luc have each ordered pizza. One has ordered a large pizza, one a medium pizza, and one a small pizza. Each pizza has a different topping—one has mushrooms, one has pepperoni, and one just has cheese. From the clues below, can you work out what size pizza they'll get and what toppings they'll have?

Louise's pizza has mushrooms on it.

Luc's pizza is bigger than Marta's.

Marta's pizza does not have any pepperoni on it.

The pizza with the mushroom topping is the smallest.

Sparkly Squares

Can you place the five gems shown below into the grid, one in each empty square, so that every horizontal row and vertical column contains five different shapes? Some are already in the correct places.

Waiter Your Turn

Follow the directions to help this robot waiter serve its customers. From "start," follow each direction (up, down, left, right) by the number of squares. R3 means you need to go right for three squares, D2 means you need to go down two squares, and so on. At what table does the robot end up?

Start

From start, move
D4, R2, D3, R2, D2, R5, U3, L6,
U4, R2, D2, R3, D4, L3, U1, L4

Pie Square

The total price for each row and column of pies is shown on the right and at the bottom. Can you work out how much each pie costs? Write each pie's price in the spaces below.

🥧	🥧	🥧	🥧	**22**
🥧	🥧	🥧	🥧	**23**
🥧	🥧	🥧	🥧	**20**
🥧	🥧	🥧	🥧	**33**
20	**27**	**28**	**23**	

Eagle Eye

Ernest the Eagle has made a nest on the ramparts of a castle, but he can't remember which one. Can you work out which castle it is by reading these clues?

The castle has a drawbridge over the moat.

The castle has a portcullis.

The tower on the right of the castle is taller than the tower on the left.

The left-hand side of the castle has an odd number of windows.

A

B

C

D

E

F

Which Way?

Which kid's map leads to the swings? Each kid's route starts at the corner square nearest to them. W3 means go west three squares; N2 means go north two squares, and so on. Use the compass to help you.

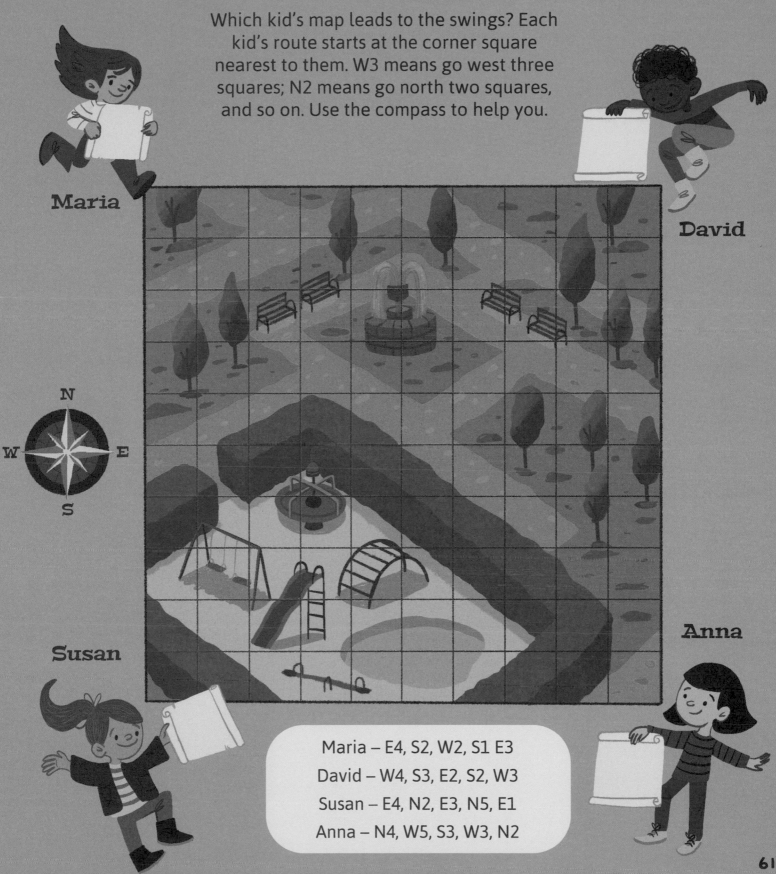

Maria

David

Susan

Anna

Maria – E4, S2, W2, S1 E3
David – W4, S3, E2, S2, W3
Susan – E4, N2, E3, N5, E1
Anna – N4, W5, S3, W3, N2

Safari So Fast

These savannah animals are having a race. Using the clues below, can you work out in which order they finished?

The giraffe finished four places behind the antelope.

The okapi finished two places ahead of the giraffe.

The rhino finished ahead of the zebra.

Busy Builder

Whitney the witch is making a stable for her unicorns. She needs 210 bricks in total, but she can't carry them all at once, so she needs to make several trips. On her first trip, she carries one brick. On the second trip, she carries two bricks. She keeps adding one brick to her load each trip until she has all the bricks she needs. In total, how many trips does she need to make?

Coin Sorter

Can you sort out these coins by placing one in each compartment so that each horizontal row and each vertical column contains five different coins?

Hop, Skippy, and Jump

Help the kangaroos cross the river by solving the equations on each stone. Stones with an answer that is an even number are safe for the kangaroos to jump on. Stones with an answer that is an odd number are too slippery and must be avoided. Can you find a path for the kangaroos to follow? Make sure they jump on every stone with an even-numbered answer.

$13 - 7$

7×3

4×8

9×9

$12 - 5$

$17 + 5$

5×4

$14 + 7$

$9 \div 3$

$18 - 10$

$6 \div 3$

$16 \div 2$

$7 + 5$

$11 + 4$

Foodie Fun

Each letter represents an item on the menu.
Compare the pictures to work out which item each
letter represents. What is the waiter asking for?

Puppy Party

If each mama dog has six puppies, how many puppies are missing from this picture?

Beary Helpful

Can you help this bear reach the honeycomb in the middle of the maze, and then go on to her den?

Start

Just Pooling Around

Can you spot 10 differences between
these two pool scenes?

Viking Valuables

Each Viking is sitting on a great big pile of gold and jewels. There's a pattern between the number of jewels in each pile. Can you work out what it is, and how many jewels should be in the sixth and final pile? Can you also work out how many jewels there are in total?

Think Your Drink

These four drinks form a sequence. Using pens, crayons, or pencils, can you complete the pattern of the final drink?

Creepy-Crawly Cubes

Which of the bug-themed cubes can be made by folding this pattern of squares?

Cookie Cutter

This cookie machine won't stop making cookies! Every minute, the number of cookies it makes doubles. In the first minute, it made two cookies. In the second minute, it made four cookies. How many cookies did the machine make in the sixth minute? How many had it made in total after seven minutes?

Traffic Stop

Can you draw paths to link these six pairs of moving machines? Each path must be made up of only vertical or horizontal lines. The paths cannot touch, and no more than one line can be in a grid square.

Big Fish

Some of these fish are big, but others are really small. Can you work out their order from biggest to smallest? Write the correct order in the spaces below. We've done one to get you started.

Card Trick

Using the playing cards below, can you make four hands each containing three different cards with values that total 10? The ace has a value of one.

Squirrel Away

This squirrel needs to collect all of these tasty treats before she hibernates for the winter. Without taking your pencil off the page, can you draw a route that collects all nine treats, but uses just four straight, continuous lines? Start the squirrel in the bottom-right corner. Your lines can overlap, as long as they do not exceed four.

Turtly Unique

These turtles look very much alike, apart from one
that has a noticeable difference. Can you spot him?

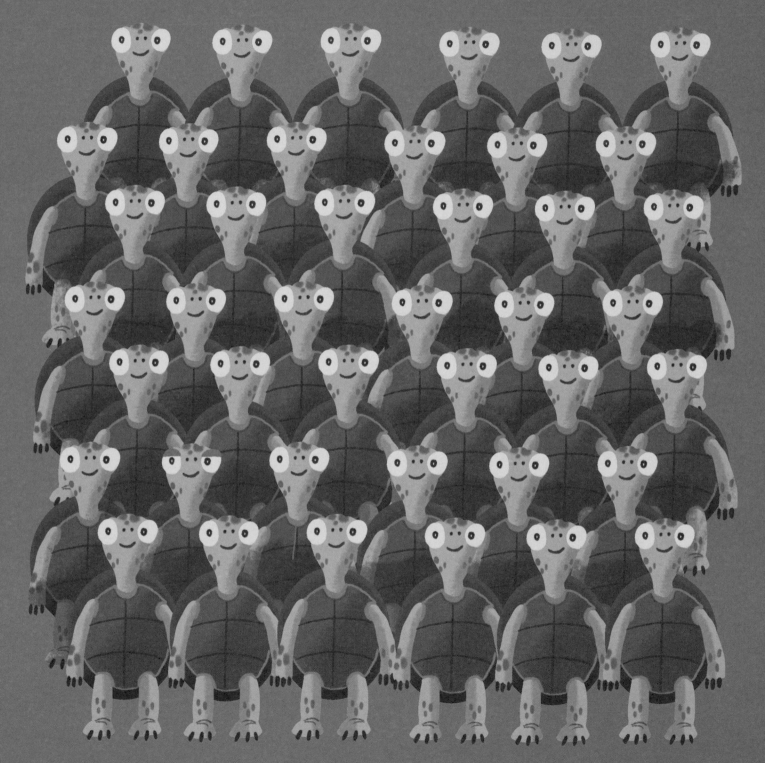

Snail's Pace

The snail is starting her journey outside the bottom-left square. Move N3, E3, N1, W3, N4, E3, S2, E4, N1, W2, N2, E4, S2, W1, S5.

This little snail is exploring a new fruit and veggie patch. Help her find her way to the plant she likes the most by following the compass directions—N3 means go north three squares. E2 means go east two squares, and so on. Which plant does she like best?

Run for the Hills

This athlete has misplaced some of her belongings.
Can you help her find the objects in this scene?

A Knight's Tale

Can you help this knight work out which of these piles of money is worth the most? One gold coin is worth ten copper pennies. Two silver coins are worth one gold coin. Convert the gold and silver coins to their equivalent values in copper coins to find the total value of each pile.

Desert Dilemma

If you fold this desert pattern to make a cube,
which of the cubes below would it match?

Egg-streme Sport

Can you repair Humpty Dumpty by identifying the correct eight pieces that make him up?

Teachers' Corner

The teachers are sorting out their spaces for the coming school year. Can you divide this page into four separate areas using just three straight lines? Each teaching area must contain a teacher, a desk and chair, and a board.

Beachy Keen

Can you spot the 10 differences between
these busy beach scenes?

Seeing Double

Can you spot one giraffe that doesn't match a reflection in the watering hole?

Answers

4. Which Witch?

5. Knight Vision

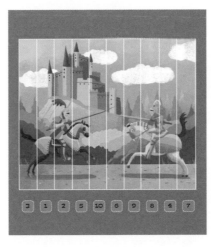

3 1 2 5 10 6 9 8 4 7

6. Bounty Aplenty

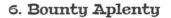

7. Just Kitten Around

The tan cat with brown spots has six kittens.

The black cat has seven kittens.

The orange and tan cat has nine kittens.

The brown striped cat has three kittens.

The grey cat has three kittens.

$6 + 7 + 9 + 3 + 3 = 28$

There are 28 kittens in total.

8. Feeding Time

Tile C does not appear in the picture.

9. Messy Mer-Kids

10. Waggy-Tail Walkers

11. Beetling About

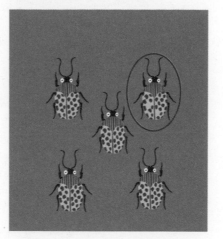

12. Putting Down Roots

One person can plant four trees per hour, so three people can plant 12 trees per hour.

In seven hours, the group will plant 84 trees.

12 x 7 = 84

13. Diving In

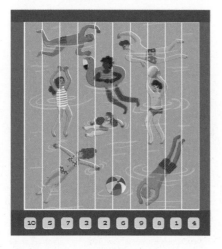

14. Toy Store Stumper

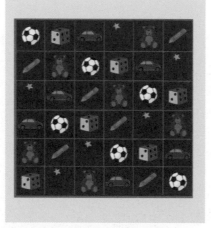

15. Model Mayhem

16. Snow Much Fun

There are 13 polar bears in the scene.

17. Puppy Pals

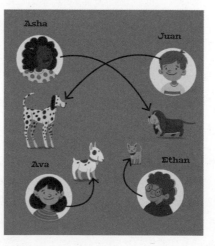

18. Alligator Snap

Tile 4 does not appear in the picture.

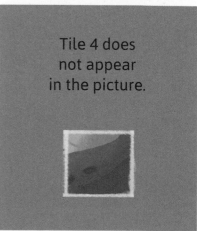

19. Monkeying Around

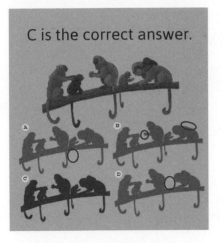

C is the correct answer.

20. Penguin Pairs

21. Dragon's Nest

There are 40 swords.

22. River Rocks

23. Can You Dig It?

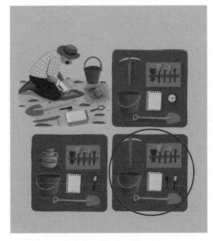

24. Adventure Bikes

25. The Butterfly Effect

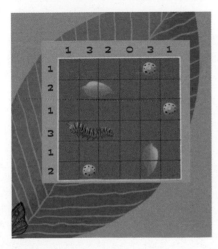

26. Wonderlost

The rabbit hole is in the Mad Hatter's house.

27. Cake Challenge

The sprinkles alternate between blue and red; the final cake has red sprinkles.

The orange tier in Cake 1 moves to the top of Cake 2, which moves the other tiers down one spot. This pattern continues until the final cake.

28. Island Hopping

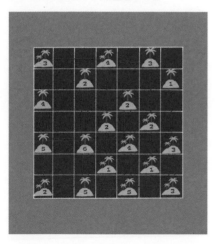

29. Crank it Up!

If you turn the green cog clockwise, the pink cog at the top will also turn clockwise.

30. Deep-Sea Spotting

Puzzle piece D is the only one that doesn't appear in the ocean scene.

31. Mayflies in Disguise

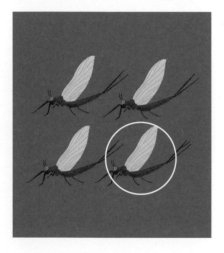

32. Puddle in the Muddle

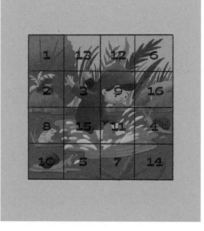

33. Mice Maze

34. Monster Mystery

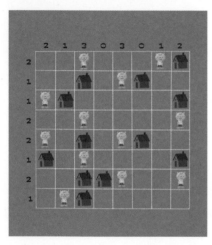

35. Star Bright

There are 20 stars jumbled together.

36. Put a Fork in It

It would take six swaps. Each time, you take a knife from the right compartment and swap it with a fork from the left compartment.

37. A Leg Up

There is a total
of 150 legs.

10 (bees) x 6 (legs) = 60
10 (spiders) x 8 (legs) = 80
5 (birds) x 2 (legs) = 10

60 + 80 + 10 = 150

38. Crowd Pleaser

39. A Tall Order

The correct order,
from tallest to
shortest, is: 4, 8, 2,
1, 9, 3, 5, 6, 7

40. Dress-Up Box

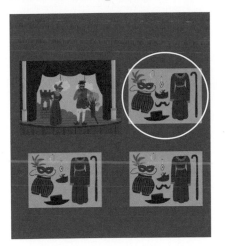

41. We Have Bake-Off!

Nico:
Chocolate pie

Kate:
Lemon layer cake

Nina:
Strawberry
cupcake

42. Tiaras in a Tangle

There are 16 tiaras
in the tangle.

43. Pairing Up

44. Track Stars

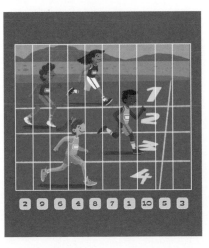

45. Busy Bees

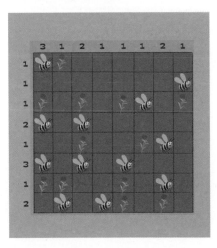

46. Bounce Out

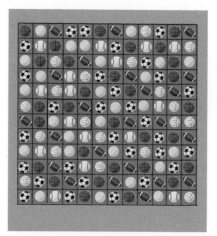

47. Day at the Museum

48. Fungi Fun

1. The sequence adds two at each stage.

2. The sequence adds three at each stage.

3. The sequence subtracts three from the previous total at each stage.

4. The sequence consists of prime numbers: 2, 3, 5, 7, 11.

49. Smitten Kitten

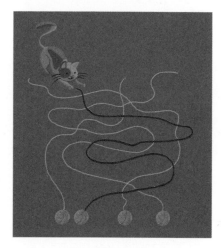

50. Maximum Load

Pile 2 is the correct answer.

Pile 1 weighs 18 feathers.

Pile 2 weighs 14 feathers.

Pile 3 weighs 16 feathers.

51. Munch a Bunch

A. The sequence adds two at each stage.

B. The sequence subtracts three from the previous total at each stage.

C. The sequence halves the previous total at each stage.

D. The sequence halves the previous total at each stage.

52. Pizzarithmetic

It will take 60 minutes to cook 17 pizzas.

53. Bangle Tangle

There are 19 bracelets in the tangle.

54. Banking Error

The circled key is still missing a label.

55. Entry Code

56. Pizza the Action

Louise's pizza is the smallest and has mushrooms.

Marta's pizza is medium sized and just has cheese.

Luc's pizza is the largest and has pepperoni.

57. Sparkly Squares

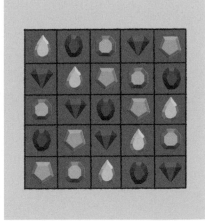

58. Waiter Your Turn

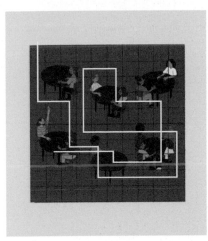

59. Pie Square

60. Eagle Eye

Ernest is meeting his friend in Castle C.

61. Which Way?

62. Safari So Fast

1 – antelope

2 – rhino

3 – okapi

4 – zebra

5 – giraffe

63. Busy Builder

She makes 20 total trips.

1 + 2 + 3 + 4 + 5 + 6 + 7 + 8 + 9 + 10 + 11 + 12 + 13 + 14 +15 + 16 + 17 + 18 + 19 + 20 = 210

64. Coin Sorter

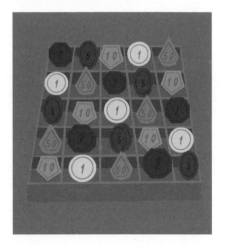

65. Hop, Skippy, and Jump

66. Foodie Fun

The waiter is asking for a cupcake and a coffee.

A = milkshake
B = cupcake
C = slice of cake
D = coffee
E = sandwich
F = banana
G = tea
H = lemon-lime soda

67. Puppy Party

There are two puppies missing: one white and one orange.

68. Beary Helpful

69. Just Pooling Around

70. Viking Valuables

The pattern is as follows:

Viking 1 has 2 jewels

Viking 2 has 5 jewels (+3)

Viking 3 has 9 jewels (+4)

Viking 4 has 14 jewels (+5)

Viking 5 has 20 jewels (+6)

Viking 6 should have 27 jewels (+7). Combined, the Vikings have 77 jewels in total.

71. Think Your Drink

The fruit wedges alternate between orange and green; the final drink has a green wedge. The top layer in the first drink moves to the middle layer in the second drink, which "bumps" the other layers down by one and into the next cup. The pattern continues until fourth drink, which looks the same as the first.

72. Creepy-Crawly Cubes

Cube A is the correct answer.

73. Cookie Cutter

In the sixth minute, the machine made 64 cookies. After 7 minutes, it had made 254 cookies in total (2 + 4 + 8 + 16 + 32 + 64 + 128 = 254)

74. Traffic Stop

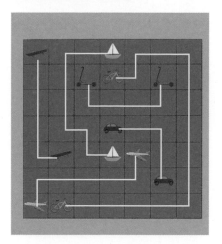

75. Big Fish

The correct order is 9, 6, 1, 2, 10, 5, 3, 4, 8, 7, 11

76. Card Trick

77. Squirrel Away

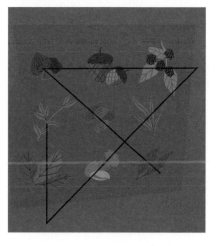

78. Turtly Unique

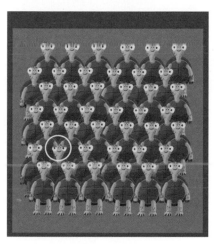

79. Snail's Pace

80. Run for the Hills

81. A Knight's Tale

Pile 4 is worth the most.

Pile 1: 2 gold, 3 silver, 7 copper = 42

Pile 2: 1 gold, 6 silver, 3 copper = 43

Pile 3: 3 gold, 11 copper = 41

Pile 4: 2 gold, 4 silver, 6 copper = 46

Pile 5: 1 gold, 5 silver, 9 copper = 44

82. Desert Dilemma

Cube C is the correct answer.

83. Egg-streme Sport

84. Teachers' Corner

85. Beachy Keen

86. Seeing Double

This giraffe doesn't have a reflection in the pond—it's too far away.